Illustrations by Paul Hess
Text by JoAnn Early Macken

Gareth Stevens Publishing
A WORLD ALMANAC EDUCATION GROUP COMPANY

9/07

Please visit our web site at: www.garethstevens.com
For a free color catalog describing Gareth Stevens Publishing's
list of high-quality books and multimedia programs,
call 1-800-542-2595 or fax your request to (414) 332-3567.

For Karen Scawen — P. H.
For The Hive, my classmates in the Vermont College MFA in Writing for Children Program — J. E. M.

Library of Congress Cataloging-in-Publication Data

Macken, JoAnn Early.
    African animals / text by JoAnn Early Macken; illustrations by Paul Hess.
       p. cm. — (Animal worlds)
    Includes bibliographical references.
    Summary: Simple text and illustrations introduce animals that live in the African grasslands,
such as the zebra, hyena, vulture, leopard, and gnu.
    ISBN 0-8368-3038-5 (lib. bdg.)
    1. Zoology—Africa—Juvenile literature. [1. Zoology—Africa.] I. Hess, Paul, ill. II. Title.
QL336.M33   2002
591.96—dc21
                                      2001054161

This North American edition first published in 2002 by
Gareth Stevens Publishing
A World Almanac Education Group Company
330 West Olive Street, Suite 100
Milwaukee, Wisconsin 53212 USA

This U.S. edition © 2002 by Gareth Stevens, Inc. First published as *Safari Animals* by Zero to Ten Limited,
a member of the Evans Publishing Group, 327 High Street, Slough, Berkshire SL1 1TX, United Kingdom.
© 1998 by Zero to Ten Ltd. Illustrations © 1996 by Paul Hess. This edition published under license from
Zero to Ten Limited. All rights reserved.

Book design: Sarah Godwin
Gareth Stevens cover design: Katherine A. Goedheer
Gareth Stevens series editor: Dorothy L. Gibbs

Printed in the United States of America

1 2 3 4 5 6 7 8 9 06 05 04 03 02

Table of Contents

African Grasslands............4

Zebra 6

Rhinoceros................8

Hyena 10

Lion....................12

Vulture 14

Leopard 16

Gnu 18

Elephant 20

More Books to Read 24

African Grasslands

The wide, open plains of Africa are called grasslands or savannas. They are covered with tall, stiff grasses. Trees and shrubs sometimes grow there, too. Many of the world's largest and fastest animals live on the African grasslands. This area has only two seasons — a dry winter and a rainy summer.

Zebra

Most zebras are black and white. Some have stripes of brown, gray, or some other color. Each zebra has its own pattern of stripes.

Rhinoceros

Huge rhinos can trot or gallop. Their horns are weapons and digging tools. They lie down and roll around in mud or dust to stay cool.

Hyena

Hyenas have long front legs and short back ones. During the day, they rest in dens or tall grass. They hunt in packs at night.

Lion

Lions live in groups called prides. They catch larger, quicker prey by hunting in teams. Roaring is one way they talk to each other.

Vulture

Vultures circle high in the sky. With wings spread wide, they search for food. They can spot a meal from many miles away.

Leopard

Leopards spend much of their lives in trees. Their long tails help them balance. A leopard's spotted coat blends in with leaves and grass.

Gnu

Gnus roam the grasslands in huge herds. Their large bodies have very thin legs. Both male and female gnus have horns and beards.

Elephant

Elephants can sleep standing up or lying down. They feel, fetch, and throw with their trunks. An elephant has only four large teeth in its mouth.

More Books to Read

Elephant Quest. Ted and Betsy Lewin
(HarperCollins Children's Books)

First Book about Animals of the Plains.
(Gareth Stevens)

Here Is the African Savanna. Madeleine
Dunphy (Hyperion Press)

I Can Draw Wild Animals. Hélène
Leroux-Hugon (Gareth Stevens)